The Black Soldier

★ ★ ★ ★ ★ ★ ★ ★ ★ ★ ★ ★ ★ ★

U.S. MILITARY HISTORY INSTITUTE

The Black Soldier

1492 TO THE PRESENT

★ ★ ★ ★ ★ ★ ★ ★ ★ ★ ★ ★ ★ ★ ★ ★ ★ ★ ★

CATHERINE CLINTON

HOUGHTON MIFFLIN COMPANY
BOSTON 2000

Copyright © 2000 by Catherine Clinton

ALL RIGHTS RESERVED. For information about permission to reproduce selections from this book, write to Permissions, Houghton Mifflin Company, 215 Park Avenue South, New York, New York 10003.

www.hmco.com/trade

The text of this book is set in Adobe Caslon.
Book design by Lisa Diercks

Library of Congress Cataloging-in-Publication Data
    Clinton, Catherine, 1952–
    The Black soldier / Catherine Clinton.
        p.   cm.
    Summary: Chronicles the military accomplishments of African Americans who fought for the independence and preservation of the United States while struggling to be treated as equals and recognized for their valor and achievement.
    ISBN 0-395-67722-X
    1. Afro-American soldiers—History—Juvenile literature. 2. United States—Armed Forces—Afro-Americans—History—Juvenile literature. [1. Afro-American soldiers—History. 2. Soldiers. 3. United States—Armed Forces—Afro-Americans—History.]
I. Title.
    E185.63.C57   2000
    355'.0089'96073—dc21   99-048935

Manufactured in the United States of America
CRW 10 9 8 7 6 5 4 3 2 1

DEDICATED TO ERIC AND DARIA FONER,

AND TO THE MEMORY OF JACK FONER,

THREE GENERATIONS OF VALOR AND TALENT

Contents

Introduction

★ ★ ★ ★ ★ ★ ★ ★ ★ ★ ★ ★

BLACKS HAVE FOUGHT AND DIED in the Americas for centuries, creating an unbroken chain of warriors stretching back nearly five hundred years. Many of these heroes, who made tremendous sacrifices to contribute to the greatness of America, lie in unmarked graves—their achievements unknown, their bravery unheralded. Nevertheless, African Americans remain prepared to do their duty, to shoulder their burdens, and to demonstrate their loyalty and talents.

African Americans took up arms whenever given the opportunity—as soldiers of fortune, as rebels, and as patriots. They have fought throughout the Americas and beyond American borders. Black warriors fought for the independence and preservation of the United States. They have risked their lives to secure freedom for their families and their people. Simultaneously, blacks have also waged a fierce struggle to be treated with dignity, to be viewed as equals, and to be recognized for their valor and achievements. Thus, their accomplishments in the military, as patriots and as freedom fighters, are too important not to be told.

Too many stories of sacrifice and courage lie buried with their bones. Yet the black soldier, in peace and war, valiantly marches on.

ONE

Exploration and Conquest in the 1500s

✴ ✴ ✴ ✴ ✴ ✴ ✴ ✴ ✴ ✴ ✴ ✴ ✴

DURING THE EARLY DAYS of transatlantic exploration, many Africans accompanied explorers on rugged sailing expeditions to "the New World," as Europeans called the Americas. Some of these Africans were "soldiers of fortune" who fought alongside Europeans. But many more were slaves captured from their African homeland and forced to work for white masters, often bundled across the sea against their will.

When Vasco Núñez de Balboa discovered the Pacific Ocean in 1513, thirty enslaved Africans were with him on this historic expedition. Hernán Cortés, conqueror of the Aztecs, took three hundred Africans on his military expedition to Mexico in 1519. When Francisco Pizarro initiated his two-year campaign to conquer Peru in 1531, he sought to capture the Incan capital of Cuzco. One of the four soldiers Pizarro handpicked to scout for this crucial mission was African-born. The name of this Spanish soldier, as well as of many other Africans whose military valor was exemplary, has been lost.

We do know the name of African-born Pedro Alonso Niño, the navigator of the *Santa Maria*, who arrived in the New World with Columbus in 1492. We also know the name of Diego Méndez, the African crew member who was with Columbus on the *Capitana* during his last voyage to the Americas in 1502.

Another African whose exploits were recorded and celebrated had an incredible adventure. He was known as Estevan or Estevanico (Little Stephen). Born in Morocco and sold into slavery by the Spaniards, Estevan set sail for the Americas with his Spanish master in 1527. Along the way, their ship encountered one disaster after another. First, a hurricane nearly destroyed the vessel and its crew. Then the seamen suffered a deadly outbreak of disease. Next they were shipwrecked along the mainland of the Gulf Coast, and North American Indians enslaved those who survived the wreck.

After several months in captivity, Estevan was able to escape his Native American captors. With three other captives, he made a daring overland trek, journeying several hundred miles before finally reaching Mexico City in 1536. An astonished Spanish viceroy welcomed the ragtag band after their incredible eight-year ordeal of searching for civilization in the wilderness. Estevan held the viceroy spellbound with his stories of survival and living off the land.

For many years European explorers known as conquistadors had been searching for the legendary Seven Cities of Gold, where treasure was supposed to be hidden in underground caves, glittering with jewels. After his adventures, Estevan was favored by the viceroy, who wanted him to seek out this treasure for Spain. In 1539, under the Spanish flag, the African explorer was sent on an expedition into what is now New Mexico. When the adventurers approached an inhabited area, Estevan scouted ahead alone, moving toward a large pueblo (an Indian dwelling built into the

Zuni Indian pueblo in what became New Mexico. CORBIS/BETTMANN

cliffs) where native people, the Zuni Indians, lived. He greeted the Zunis in a friendly manner—offering a peace gourd decorated with bells and colorful feathers—to demonstrate his friendship. Despite his gesture of goodwill, the Indians mistrusted this stranger, as the Spanish had been there before and many Indians had died as a result. The telltale Spanish bells gave Estevan away: Europeans had sent him. Estevan died at the hands of his captors. When the Zuni Indians rode out from their pueblo, the rest of Estevan's expedition party fled, barely escaping with their lives. They returned to the viceroy in Mexico to report on their leader's sad fate.

Estevan was one of hundreds of Africans who joined the ranks of European armies of conquest, but one of only a handful whose accomplishments and experiences were recorded for future generations.

TWO

The Colonial Era
1600–1769

★ ★ ★ ★ ★ ★ ★ ★ ★ ★ ★ ★ ★

IN THE SEVENTEENTH CENTURY, Europeans were desperate for people willing to sail across the Atlantic to live and work in their overseas outposts, settlements known as colonies. The Portuguese were building an empire in Brazil. The Spanish wanted settlers for outposts in Central and South America, as well as for colonies in Florida. The Dutch, French, and English competed to settle islands in the Caribbean, as well as along the coast of North America.

Poor whites were shipped to these settlements as indentured servants—persons who exchanged their labor for passage to the New World. They were expected to work for a master for a number of years before being freed from their contract. Once they were free, they could farm their own land.

Africans were stolen or sold from their homelands and shipped to the New World without any promise of eventual freedom; this system was known as slavery. Slavery was common throughout the islands of the Caribbean and was introduced into mainland North America in Virginia as early as 1619.

Even though Europeans were settling in a hostile region, they feared letting the "salt backs"—as newly arrived Africans were called—have weapons.

White colonists were afraid that the slaves might use the guns against them in a rebellion to gain their freedom. However, the constant threat of attack by Indians along the Atlantic frontier caused blacks and whites to band together. Soldiers, free and enslaved, stood as sentries for colonial settlements, and many slave soldiers were the allies of their masters, protecting their homes from Indian attacks.

As early as 1652, a law in Massachusetts allowed Africans to be trained by the local militia. When five Indian tribes united during the 1670s, they waged war throughout the New England colonies under the leadership of a Wampanoag chief who became known as King Philip. After losing nearly three thousand warriors, the Indians were defeated in what came to be known as King Philip's War. During this fierce contest, the Indians wiped out twelve towns in the English colonies, and more than six hundred settlers died, including Africans who had fought alongside their masters.

In 1715 African Americans fought with the militia on the South Carolina frontier during the bloody Yamassee War, driving Carolina Indians back from the boundary so that planters and farmers could expand their settlements westward.

But not all blacks fought alongside their masters. Some enslaved Africans stole their owners' weapons—and they even "stole themselves," becoming runaways. Permanent runaways were known as maroons and lived in outlaw settlements. These fugitives formed independent communities, hiding in swamps and other isolated regions, away from white settlers. Maroons fought hard to live independently and to avoid being captured and returned to slavery.

In the Mississippi Delta, the French created coastal outposts in order to ship valuable goods back to Europe. They also imported African slaves (Ibo, Fulani, and other West African nations) to harvest sugar cane, clear timber, and perform other backbreaking labor. One rebel among them gained great fame. Born in the kingdom of Gambia, St. Malo was taken into slavery and shipped to Louisiana by the French. He ran away and led a band of maroons who eventually took control of the bayou (the region where the Mississippi River meets the Gulf of Mexico). To warn Europeans who might want to recapture slaves, St. Malo once drove an axe into a tree and dared any white man to defy him with a sign that read:

MALHEUR AU BLANCS QUI PASSERA CES BORNES.
(WOE TO THE WHITES WHO WOULD PASS THIS BOUNDARY.)

St. Malo became so renowned that French authorities gathered a large force of soldiers to capture him. He was eventually hunted down and hanged in 1784. His legendary exploits are still celebrated in folklore among Louisiana Creoles.

One of the most intrepid black military leaders of the colonial period was Francisco Menéndez, an enslaved Mandingo warrior in South Carolina who led a band of fugitive slaves southward into Florida and to freedom. In 1738 this African slave rebel founded Fort Mosa, the first free black settlement on the North American continent. This community of former slaves pledged its allegiance to the Spanish Crown. The Spanish governor granted protection to its inhabitants, who all converted to Catholicism.

Menéndez's heroic exodus was perhaps the inspiration for the most famous slave rebellion in the English settlements during the colonial era. One fateful night in September 1739, two dozen Africans gathered at a creek bed near the Stono River in South Carolina. It was there that Jemmy, a slave born in Angola, encouraged his fellow bondsmen to rise up against their masters and flee to Florida.

Soon the rebels began to chant "liberty" and, caught up in the spirit, followed Jemmy into the night. They burned, looted, and even murdered as they marched southward, growing to nearly one hundred strong by dawn. The next day, shortly before noon, white militiamen caught up with these black freedom fighters. Although outnumbered and outgunned, the slave rebels fought courageously.

The Stono Rebellion, as this event became known, was over by sundown; all the rebels were killed, or they had escaped or surrendered. But rumors of a conspiracy ricocheted throughout the countryside for many years, as the cry for freedom swept through slave communities up and down the Atlantic seaboard.

THREE

Struggles for Independence 1770–1789

★ ★ ★ ★ ★ ★ ★ ★ ★ ★ ★ ★ ★

DURING THE 1770S, BRITISH colonists struggled against the restrictions imposed on them by England, the mother country. They felt that the burdens they shouldered were unfair, and they protested. As the conflict escalated, their leaders declared independence, organized the Continental army, and launched a war against England, calling themselves patriots and rebels.

During what became known as the American Revolution, African Americans were divided. In November 1775 Lord Dunmore, the British royal governor of Virginia, proclaimed: "I do hereby further declare all indented servants, Negroes, or others, free that are able and willing to bear arms, they joining His Majesty's Troops." Many African Americans took this chance to gain freedom and supported the Crown.

But from the earliest days of conflict with the British authorities, African Americans were also at the forefront of the move for independence. Crispus Attucks, the first and one of the most famous heroes of the Revolution, was the son of an African father, John Attucks, and an Indian mother. In the autumn of 1750, when Attucks fled his master, the *Boston Gazette* reported: "Ran away from his Master William Brown of Framingham . . . a Molatto Fellow, about 27 years of Age. Names Crispas 6 feet two Inches high, short curl'd hair." Little else is known about him, except for the kind of clothes he wore when he ran away. Attucks blended in with the free black community in Boston and was not heard from again until the mobbing of the British Customs House on March 5, 1770. Five protesters were shot by British soldiers known as redcoats, in a tragic skirmish called the Boston Massacre. Of the five patriots shot that day, Attucks was the first to fall. Ever since, he has been celebrated as the first hero to die for American independence.

In May 1775 only free blacks were welcomed into George Washington's Continental army. As the war dragged on, eventually slaves were allowed to serve in the military and were even given their freedom if they enlisted. Between six thousand and eight thousand African Americans fought against the British to help win the American Revolution.

British troops, known as Tories, taunted the rebels with songs about black soldiers:

> *The rebel clowns, oh what a sight*
> *Too awkward was their figure*
> *Twas yonder stood a pious wight*
> *And here and there a nigger.*

Despite the ridicule, African American soldiers proved themselves in battle. Salem Poor had been born a slave in Framingham, Massachusetts, but as a soldier in the Continental army, he distinguished himself by shooting British commander Major John Pitcairn at a critical moment in the decisive Battle of Bunker Hill in Boston. Poor's commanding officer

This eighteenth-century illustration depicts the Boston Massacre, where Crispus Attucks died. CORBIS/BETTMANN

commended him as a "Brave & Gallant Soldier" after his valiant perform-ance in one of the war's earliest encounters.

On Christmas Eve in 1776, when General Washington launched a dar-ing surprise attack by rowing his troops across a river in the dead of night, winning the Battle of Trenton, he was accompanied by the slave Prince Whipple and many other African Americans.

There were several other black heroes during the Revolutionary War. When British soldiers landed to burn the towns of Groton and New London, Connecticut, Lambert Latham joined the battle at Fort Griswold. His commander, Colonel William Ledyard, surrendered, offering the British commander his sword. But the British officer drove the blade through Ledyard. After Ledyard's death, Latham continued fighting, and was mobbed by British soldiers who stabbed him repeatedly with their bayonets. Latham died of his thirty-three wounds.

George Washington crossed the Delaware with African American Prince Whipple under his command. CORBIS/BETTMANN

Fourteen-year-old free black James Forten was a powder boy on the American ship *Royal Louis*. He was captured by the British and offered his freedom, but Forten refused, declaring: "I'm a prisoner for my country and I'll never be a traitor to her." The young boy served seven months on a prison ship.

James Armistead, a Virginia slave, convinced the British commander Charles Cornwallis that he would spy for him. Instead, Armistead became a double agent! He reported British troop movements and other important information to French general Lafayette, who fought with the Continental army. Armistead's espionage "at the peril of his life" (as a later commendation read) contributed to American victory at Yorktown and British surrender in 1781.

Sadly, in a pattern that was to be repeated, African American soldiers were welcomed in the trenches but not at victory dinners. One black veteran complained that he was "looked for in the 'hour of danger' but trampled underfoot in time of peace." In addition, soldiers of color did not receive their share of bounties (parcels of land offered to soldiers as a reward for their service to their country) and pensions. Some even had to fight off former masters who tried to reenslave them once the war was over.

After the American Revolution, blacks, even veterans of the Continental army, were disqualified from enrolling in state militias. In 1792 Congress passed a law restricting military service to "able-bodied white males." William Watkins angrily complained: "When we petition for the right to be enrolled in the military companies in the state of Massachusetts, we are told our complexion is 'unconstitutional.'"

Black soldiers had fought long and hard for the victory of American independence and the promise of a new nation. As for freedom and independence for themselves, many African Americans feared they would have an even harder battle ahead.

FOUR

Struggles for Freedom
1790–1860

★ ★ ★ ★ ★ ★ ★ ★ ★ ★ ★ ★ ★

WHEN THE UNITED STATES WENT to war against the British in the War of 1812, once again whites abandoned race prejudice temporarily to encourage both free and enslaved blacks to defend the nation from enemy attack. And African Americans did take up arms—again, on both sides of the conflict.

As in the Revolutionary War, the British made promises to American slaves, trying to persuade them to desert their masters and join the British army. In the spring of 1813 the British recruited an entire company of black marines off plantations in the Chesapeake Bay region (Virginia and Maryland).

At the same time, African Americans volunteered by the hundreds to serve loyally as American soldiers. In 1813 black sailors fought with Commodore Perry at the Battle of Lake Erie, and on the Louisiana frontier black soldiers volunteered to follow General Andrew Jackson. During the heroic victory at the Battle of New Orleans in 1815, Jackson commended the black warriors under his command: "I invited you to share in the perils of your white countrymen. I expected much from you. . . . But you surpass my hopes; I have found in you . . . that noble enthusiasm which impels to great deeds."

Black soldiers joined whites in the Battle of New Orleans. CORBIS/BETTMANN

Black veterans of the War of 1812, like their Revolutionary forefathers, were disappointed at war's end. Their wartime loyalty and service did not translate into opportunities during peacetime. This was a harsh lesson for black soldiers, especially when the curtain of race prejudice came down again in 1820 and the War Department declared: "No Negro or Mulatto will be received as a recruit of the Army."

After defeating the British in 1815, the United States wanted to expand its borders. Americans stampeded the frontier. Southward and westward, white settlers claimed new lands, many of them with slaves in tow.

U.S. soldiers who crossed the Rio Grande along the country's south-western border became involved in the U.S.-Mexican War (1846–1848), which won more land for the growing nation.

Antislavery feelings were on the rise, and African Americans realized that patriotism and military accomplishments alone could not break the shackles of slavery, which kept most black Americans in bondage. Increasingly, they took matters into their own hands. Free black or slave leaders who encouraged slave rebellions most often died a martyr's death. These rebels were heroes to many African Americans—freedom fighters who died for the cause of black freedom, striking a blow against slavery.

Gabriel Prosser was a free black in Richmond, Virginia, a blacksmith by trade, who in the summer of 1800 conspired to lead an uprising of slaves and poor whites banded together. Many slaves in the countryside had hidden pikes and axes in preparation for their insurrection. The night the revolt was scheduled to begin, however, floods prevented them from reaching rebel headquarters. The plot was betrayed, and scores of blacks were arrested, including Prosser, who was hanged on October 7, 1800.

In Charleston, South Carolina, free black Denmark Vesey, who had been variously a sailor, a carpenter, and a preacher, gained his freedom when he won enough money in a local lottery to purchase himself from his master. He went on to become a local leader and inspired others to seek their own freedom. Vesey urged fellow blacks to rise up and liberate slaves, but his plan for revolt was betrayed as well. Although Vesey escaped armed search parties for two days, eventually he was caught, put on trial, and found guilty of organizing a slave rebellion. Vesey was hanged on July 2, 1822.

The third and most famous leader of a slave revolt in America took a very different path. Nat Turner, a literate and deeply religious man, was a

HORRID MASSACRE IN VIRGINIA.

The Scenes which the above Plate is designed to represent, are—Fig. 1. a Mother intreating for the lives of her children.—2. Mr. Travis, cruelly murdered by his own Slaves.—3. Mr. Barrow, who bravely defended himself until his wife escaped.—4. A comp. of mounted Dragoons in pursuit of the Blacks.

Nat Turner led the most famous slave revolt of the nineteenth century.

LIBRARY OF CONGRESS

slave in Southampton County, Virginia, who served as a preacher and a prophet to his fellow slaves. On the night of August 22, 1831, he urged them to rise up and cast off their chains.

That fateful night, this band of eighty slave rebels moved from house to house, murdering most of the whites they encountered. The local militiamen responded to an alarm and quickly moved to crush the revolt—but not before the rebels had killed more than fifty whites.

Most of the rebels were caught the next day, although Nat Turner evaded a manhunt for weeks. He was finally captured on October 31. After a hasty trial, the leader of the largest slave revolt in American history was condemned to death and hanged on November 11. Nat Turner has become a folkloric figure for many African Americans.

During the decades leading up to the Civil War, fugitive slaves headed to Canada by the hundreds—along routes that became known as the Underground Railroad. This network was neither a railroad nor underground but a secret system of transportation and safe houses for moving fugitives from slavery to freedom. Large numbers of free blacks volunteered to serve in this clandestine and dangerous operation.

The North Star became a symbol of freedom to fugitive slaves as they followed this bright beacon to safety. The *North Star* was also the name of the antislavery newspaper edited by black leader Frederick Douglass. Born a slave, Douglass had fled his master, bought his own freedom, and become an abolitionist and lecturer in his hometown of Rochester, New York. He joined with hundreds of blacks and whites in the battle against slavery, the fight for abolitionism.

John Brown, a white abolitionist, decided to invade the South and incite slaves to revolt. On October 16, 1859, he led a band of twenty-two men in an attack on a federal arsenal at Harpers Ferry, Virginia. Five blacks joined Brown on this ill-fated military assault. Those who did not die in the raid were captured and put on trial. Many were hanged for their role in the attempted insurrection, including African American John

Frederick Douglass, himself a former slave, became the most famous black leader of his day. LIBRARY OF CONGRESS

John Brown enlisted blacks as well as whites during his 1859 armed attack in Virginia. LIBRARY OF CONGRESS

Copeland. Copeland wrote following his capture: "I am not terrified by the gallows, which I see staring me in the face, and upon which I am soon to stand and suffer death for doing what George Washington was made a hero for doing."

After John Brown's raid, conflicts over slavery escalated. Many believed that slavery was an issue worth fighting for, and blacks as well as whites concluded that the debate could be settled only by force.

FIVE

The Civil War and Its Legacy 1861–1877

★ ★ ★ ★ ★ ★ ★ ★ ★ ★ ★ ★ ★ ★

WHEN THE NORTH AND THE South went to war, African Americans volunteered without hesitation. Blacks organized Union regiments in Kansas and South Carolina, responding to President Lincoln's call to arms following the attack on Fort Sumter in April 1861.

At the same time, in the South, a militia composed of free men of color, known as the New Orleans Native Guards, volunteered to join the Confederate army. Many free blacks in the South remained loyal to their states. Members of Charleston's Brown Society, a group of mixed-race free blacks, sent a letter to the governor of South Carolina pledging their loyalty: "Our attachments are with you, our hopes of safety and protection from you. Our allegiance is due to South Carolina, and in her defense we are willing to offer up our lives, and all that's dear to us." However, this was a rare example of African American allegiance to the Confederate cause. The overwhelming majority of black Americans, free and slave, supported the Union cause. Ironically, when war broke out, both the federal government and the Confederate army refused black military volunteers, even those slaves who organized behind enemy lines to fight for the North.

African Americans in the North championed the cause of the black soldier. Frederick Douglass devoted a lot of time and energy to it, believing that military service would ease the road to racial justice: "Let the black man get upon his person the brass letters U.S., let him get an eagle on his button and a musket on his shoulder. There is no power on earth which can deny that he earned the right to citizenship in the United States."

African American leaders sent petitions to Lincoln begging him to allow black soldiers to fight. They also urged him to abolish slavery, to hurt the Confederates by freeing their slaves. After much debate within his government, Lincoln finally decided to let African Americans serve in the military and to abolish slavery in the Rebel states. Lincoln made his announcement in September 1862, and his decision became law on January 1, 1863. The Emancipation Proclamation freed the slaves of Rebel masters and paved the way for growing numbers of blacks to enter the Union army. Union commander Ulysses S. Grant welcomed this development and argued: "By arming the Negro, we have added a powerful ally. They will make good soldiers and taking them from the enemy weakens him in the same proportion they strengthen us."

The Confederates announced they would not treat blacks as soldiers. They angrily declared that any blacks in Union uniform would be treated as "insurrectionists" and shot on sight, with no prisoners taken. This terrible threat hung over every black Union soldier.

African American soldiers in the Union army were segregated, and only white officers were placed in charge of colored troops. One officer in charge of training raw black recruits complained of the constant scrutiny:

"I felt sometimes as if we were a plant trying to take root, but constantly pulled up to see if we were growing."

In May 1863 some of the first black Union soldiers sent into combat fought at the Battle of Port Hudson, near Vicksburg, Mississippi. The *New York Tribune* reported on this historic occasion: "The deeds of heroism performed by these colored men were such as the proudest white man might emulate." Equally impressive was the performance of black troops at the Battle of Milliken's Bend on June 6, 1863, when 200 white soldiers and 1,000 black soldiers (in uniform less than three weeks) held off an attack by 2,000 Confederate troops at a small outpost in Louisiana, fighting in hand-to-hand combat until Union warships could rescue them. Their Union commander reported, "It is impossible for men to show greater bravery than the Negro troops in that fight."

Black soldiers often sang while going into battle. A popular fighting song reflects their noble spirit:

So rally, boys, rally.
Let us never mind the past,
We had a hard road to travel
But our day is coming fast.
For God is for the right
And we have no need to fear.
The union must be saved
By the colored volunteer.

Even more heroic and more widely reported in the press were the battle exploits of the Massachusetts 54th Regiment, a segregated unit under the

The heroic charge at Fort Wagner, where scores of black soldiers lost their lives.
U.S. MILITARY HISTORY INSTITUTE

command of white officer Robert Gould Shaw, the son of a wealthy Boston abolitionist family. Shaw's men hoped to capture Fort Wagner, South Carolina, during a campaign launched in July 1863. After months of anxiously sitting on the sidelines, this African American regiment was given an opportunity to prove itself. Shaw's troops courageously led the charge to capture the Confederate stronghold. But by the end of the day, Shaw lay dead, and more than 1,500 of his men perished as well.

When a soldier fell carrying the Massachusetts 54th Regimental colors during this battle, Sergeant William Carney retrieved the flag and, although wounded several times, carried it to the top of a rampart, calling out to his fellow soldiers, "The old flag never touched the ground, boys." For his heroism, Carney became the first African American to be nominated for the Congressional Medal of Honor (awarded in 1900, thirty-seven years after his commendation). The black troops at Fort Wagner demonstrated the valor that African Americans frequently displayed as they fought for their country and against slavery, for their honor and against racism.

Harriet Tubman, a leading abolitionist, had been a witness to the charge. A heroine of the Underground Railroad, Tubman returned in 1861 from her home in Canada to help the Union effort. By 1863, she was a scout and spy for the Second Carolina Volunteers, moving behind enemy lines and leading raids on ammunition depots and plantation storehouses. In the summer of 1863, under her guidance, Union commanders liberated more than eight hundred slaves along the Combahee River in South Carolina. At Fort Wagner, she reported poetically: "And then we saw the lightning, and that was the guns; and then we heard the thunder, and that was the big guns; and then we heard the rain falling, and that was the drops of blood falling; and when we came to get the crops, it was dead men we reaped."

Six hundred black survivors of the Massachusetts 54th Regiment collected nearly $2,800 to contribute toward a memorial to be erected on Boston Common to commemorate Shaw's courage and death.

Black soldiers in combat faced dangers greater than those for white

Sergeant William Carney, whose bravery at Fort Wagner earned him the Medal of Honor. U.S. MILITARY HISTORY INSTITUTE

Harriet Tubman served as both a scout and spy for the Union army.

LIBRARY OF CONGRESS

comrades. As Confederate losses mounted, bitterness at former slaves in uniform grew. Confederates reportedly began to enforce a policy of taking no African American prisoners on several occasions, including the Saltville Massacre of October 2, 1864, in which 160 white Union soldiers were killed and 80 white Union soldiers were wounded. At the same time, 150 black Union men were killed, and only 6 black soldiers survived their wounds.

A particularly bitter struggle took place on April 12, 1864, when Confederate general Nathan Bedford Forrest launched a ferocious assault to recapture Fort Pillow, Tennessee. Only 24 of the 262 black soldiers who fought at Fort Pillow survived the battle. Eyewitnesses claimed that Confederate soldiers made good on their bloody threats—killing any black in uniform on sight. Eli Carlton, a black soldier in the Union army, told of being shot point-blank by a Rebel soldier while he lay in a hospital. Carlton survived to testify that he had witnessed dozens of black prisoners being slaughtered. For months to come black soldiers hollered "Remember Fort Pillow" before going into battle to fight the Confederates.

As early as July 30, 1863, the Union declared: "The government of the United States will give the same protection to all its soldiers." This was a measure of support for black troops, and the Union army refused to exchange prisoners if Confederates threatened to deny colored troops the rights that were extended to all other soldiers, especially the right to surrender.

Despite claims of equal protection, the Union army segregated African American recruits into separate units and offered them lower wages. When blacks were recruited for the Union army, white soldiers were paid $10 a month, and black soldiers received only $7. Colored troops patriotically did not go on strike for equal wages, but many refused to draw any earnings until they were given equal pay. This was their protest against inequality. As a result, black men in the Massachusetts 54th Regiment went without wages for almost a year. Finally, the government was forced to meet their dignified demands. Black Union troops had shamed the federal government into giving them fair pay.

Many blacks succeeded on the front lines of battles, and others triumphed behind the scenes. Robert Smalls was a trusted slave pilot whose ship, *The Planter*, ferried supplies from Charleston, South Carolina, to Fort Sumter for the Confederate army. On the night of May 13, 1862, Smalls and his crew secretly gathered their families on shipboard and made a daring escape. Hoisting a white flag at dawn and steering their Confederate ship toward Union boats guarding the harbor, they surrendered a valuable cache of weapons, as well as their most important prize, the boat itself. Congress authorized a $20,000 reward for Smalls and his men. Smalls was drafted by the Union navy and eventually rose to the rank of captain.

Another daring agent behind the lines was Mary Elizabeth Bowser, a black woman who had been born a slave in Virginia but was a free black in Philadelphia when the war broke out. Bowser was recruited by her former mistress, Virginian Elizabeth Van Lew, to return to the Rebel capital of Richmond to spy in the home of Confederate president Jefferson Davis. Working within the Confederate White House under the name of Ellen Bond, Bowser collected military secrets, at times smuggling out coded messages on dress patterns.

Black sailors served in the Union navy in large numbers. U.S. NAVAL HISTORICAL CENTER

By the time Confederate general Robert E. Lee surrendered at Appomattox Courthouse, Virginia, in April 1865, blacks had fought in 449 military engagements. African American sailors had made up nearly one-fourth of the Union navy, and more than 186,000 black soldiers had served in sixteen Union regiments, participating in thirty-nine major battles. With the peace, most blacks retired from military service, although the battle for equality, especially in the United States military, continued.

African American soldiers proved themselves time and again during the Civil War. Many moved out of the cotton fields and onto the killing fields with only a few weeks' preparation, and they demonstrated courage and determination, which won over their commanders. After the Civil War, for the first time large numbers of African Americans remained in the military. It was also the first time black soldiers had fought in a war to end slavery. This was an important legacy for the black soldier in America.

SIX

Buffalo Soldiers
1877–1918

✫ ✫ ✫ ✫ ✫ ✫ ✫ ✫ ✫ ✫ ✫ ✫

IN 1865, WITH THE COUNTRY officially reunited, African Americans began pushing for their full and equal rights during a period known as Reconstruction. While blacks in politics were struggling for equality, blacks in the military were fighting for their rights. Soldiers who remained in the army faced blatant discrimination. Often, when black troops appeared at western forts, they were told by local white commanders to camp outside the posts. In 1877, when General William T. Sherman attempted to end segregation in the army, the bill was defeated in Congress.

In the same year, Henry O. Flipper became the first African American to earn his degree and second lieutenant's bars from West Point, the U.S. military academy. Flipper recalled that when he entered the military school he was subjected to jeers and insults, but he endured all hazing with dignity. When he finally graduated (six black cadets before him had dropped out without finishing), he received enthusiastic applause and congratulations from fellow cadets, commenting, "All signs of ostracism were gone." Flipper was assigned to one of four black military units maintained in peacetime. During a time known as the Indian Wars, all of the African American troops were stationed at posts west of the Mississippi, most in

Henry Flipper, the first black graduate of West Point, in his cadet uniform.

U.S. MILITARY ACADEMY, WEST POINT, NEW YORK

Buffalo Soldiers on the Montana frontier. MONTANA HISTORICAL SOCIETY

the western territories. On this western frontier, one out of every five cavalrymen (soldiers assigned to horseback units) was black. The Native
Americans nicknamed the black fighting force Buffalo Soldiers.

At the Battle of Little Big Horn in June 1876, one of the most famous
battles of the Indian Wars, there were no Buffalo Soldiers, as Civil War
veteran General George Armstrong Custer refused to command black
troops. Custer led the men of the Seventh Cavalry into a disastrous
encounter with the Sioux. Isaiah Dorman, an interpreter for the U.S.
Army, was the only African American at the massacre, which became
known as Custer's Last Stand. The general and all 250 of his men perished.
The Sioux knew Dorman, considering him a friend, although they called
him "the black white man." When they discovered that Dorman was

Buffalo Soldiers in the 1890s. MONTANA HISTORICAL SOCIETY

wounded, the Sioux tried to revive him, but he died along with the rest of his regiment.

Conditions on the western frontier were brutal for most Buffalo Soldiers. Flipper recalled a hard life there. On one occasion he rode over thirty miles with his white orderly to inspect and receive cattle from a trail drive. When he was given a bed in a local boarding house, white trail bosses complained about the "nigger officer." Flipper ignored racist taunts, went about his business, and rode back another thirty miles with his herd, mostly in the snow. At the end of this particularly difficult journey, he had to cut his boots off his swollen feet.

Buffalo Soldiers were sent to the most inhospitable posts the army had

Buffalo Soldiers mounted for parade. U.S. MILITARY ACADEMY, WEST POINT, NEW YORK

to offer. Frank Puller, another black soldier, was stationed with the 25th Infantry in Missoula, Montana. He described the heat, which was as bad as the cold: "In winter, which lasts five months or more, the temperature falls as low as 55 degrees below zero, and in summer rises to over 100 degrees in the shade."

The military neglected these hard-working soldiers in other ways as well. Unlike white soldiers, they were not issued regimental flags and had to make their own. In 1870 a captain with the Tenth Cavalry complained that for three years "this regiment has received nothing but broken down horses and repaired equipment."

Despite obstacles, Buffalo Soldiers adjusted to their challenging environments. Some were even able to distinguish themselves in their military careers. In 1880 George Jordan, a Buffalo Soldier in New Mexico, rode through the night with two dozen black troops to defend a white settlement from an impending Apache raid. When the Apaches attacked, their braves outnumbered the black soldiers by four to one. But Jordan and his men fought off the attack and saved the day, which won Jordan the Congressional Medal of Honor, a rare accomplishment for any soldier, especially a black one.

Only a handful of whites recognized the talents and contributions of the Buffalo Soldiers, but those who did lavished praise on them. One white officer reported, "Their zeal is untiring, and if they do not always achieve success, they always deserve it. I have never seen troops more constantly employed." Another white officer, John J. Pershing—an extraordinary soldier working his way up the ladder of command—became so fond of his African American troops that he was known as "Black Jack."

By the closing decades of the nineteenth century, the need for Buffalo Soldiers to protect whites from Indian attacks was diminishing. However, this tradition continued into the next century, and the last armed clash between black troops and Indians took place along the Mexican border of Arizona in 1918, marking the end of an era.

SEVEN

The Spanish-American War, 1898

☆ ☆ ☆ ☆ ☆ ☆ ☆ ☆ ☆ ☆ ☆ ☆

DURING THE 1890S, THE United States took great interest in Cuba, a Spanish colony only ninety miles off the coast of Florida. The American government wanted to purchase Cuba (just as it had bought Alaska from Russia in 1867), but the Spanish refused to sell the island or to grant the Cubans their independence. In 1895, following a failed revolt, nearly four hundred thousand Cubans died of disease and starvation in government camps.

In February 1898, President William McKinley dispatched the U.S. battleship *Maine* to Havana Harbor. When the vessel exploded under mysterious circumstances, Congress and McKinley declared war on Spain in April, shipping American soldiers to both Cuba and the Philippines— another Spanish colony—to fight the Spanish and liberate their colonies from Spanish oppression. "Remember the *Maine*" became the Americans' battle cry. This was the first conflict in which black soldiers were officially enlisted to fight on foreign soil.

General "Black Jack" Pershing, a rising military hero, reported, "White Regiments, black regiments, regulars and Rough Riders (troops on horseback), representing the young manhood of the North and

A veteran of the Spanish-American War.

U.S. MILITARY

HISTORY INSTITUTE

Black soldiers in the Philippines. U.S. MILITARY HISTORY INSTITUTE

South, fought shoulder to shoulder, unmindful of whether commanded by an ex-Confederate or not, and mindful only of their common duty as Americans."

Twenty-two black sailors were among the American servicemen killed on the *Maine.* Teddy Roosevelt, a former secretary of the navy and future president, who had organized a voluntary unit of cavalry soldiers to fight in Cuba, called his African American cavalrymen Smoked Yankees. Black soldiers distinguished themselves at the Battle of San Juan Hill, where

American troops fought ferociously to charge up against a wall of Spanish soldiers and on to victory.

American forces also fought the Spanish in Puerto Rico and in the Philippines. Commodore George Dewey's victory at the Battle of Manila Bay sealed U.S. victory over Spain. Rough Rider Frank Knox (who later would become U.S. secretary of the navy) proudly served alongside the Tenth Cavalry, a unit of colored troops, at San Juan Hill. He observed, "I must say I never saw braver men anywhere. Some of those who rushed up the hill will live in my memory forever." During the fight with Spain, which lasted less than four months, five African Americans won the Congressional Medal of Honor.

Back at home, Americans were made aware of the courage and distinction of black soldiers. Yet racism within the ranks still disturbed African Americans. And when they were shipped back home, even the white press pointed out the unfairness black soldiers still faced. An article in the *New York Tribune* in 1898 commented: "They knew how to fight for the United States with the best of soldiers, that they could march and suffer and die with white men, even if they couldn't ride in the same car [streetcar]."

So despite yet another war, and despite yet another handful of Congressional Medal of Honor winners, at the turn of the twentieth century black soldiers continued to view race prejudice as their greatest enemy in times of peace and war.

EIGHT

Achievements and Setbacks 1898–1917

★ ★ ★ ★ ★ ★ ★ ★ ★ ★ ★ ★ ★

AT THE TURN OF THE CENTURY black soldiers had to be pioneers to advance their military careers. All branches of the military still treated African Americans as second-class citizens—segregated and limited in their opportunities. For instance, the National Guard, which was authorized to organize state militias beginning in 1903, not only enforced segregation but also allowed the exclusion of blacks in some southern states. Further, the U.S. Marine Corps refused to allow blacks to serve within its ranks.

Nevertheless, a handful of black men carved out outstanding careers for themselves. Charles Young, the third black graduate of West Point (1889), was a military instructor at Wilberforce University in Ohio, a predominantly black college, when the Spanish-American War broke out. Young served first in Cuba, then in the Philippines, where he earned the nickname "Follow Me" because of his constant bravery in the face of danger. Indeed, he inspired his troops, and his men were willing to follow him anywhere. Young became one of the first black officers in the U.S. military.

Benjamin O. Davis Sr., a graduate of Howard University, joined the army as a private and worked his way up the military ladder to become an officer. He had grown up in Washington, D.C., and was shocked by Jim

Charles Young, as a young man. U.S. MILITARY HISTORY INSTITUTE

Crow when his unit was stationed in the segregated South. (After the war, racial segregation would become known informally as Jim Crow, after a black vaudeville character. Legislation passed to enforce segregation were called Jim Crow laws.)

Transferred to Georgia, Davis and his men encountered signs at the railroad depot that read Whites and Colored. They were jostled and spat at by whites, who ignored their uniforms and saw only the color of their skin. Davis was deeply distressed by this experience and commented: "Much of my patriotism was dampened." Despite this Davis performed with heroism in Cuba and was promoted to the rank of second lieutenant and posted to the Philippines.

Both Young and Davis overcame enormous obstacles to achieve officer status and to pursue active military careers. They endured much to earn promotion and stay within the ranks, where color was viewed as a handicap for advancement.

Even though men like Young and Davis were able to move up within the segregated army, the average black soldier faced discrimination and inferior conditions. Soldiers garrisoned at southern forts experienced the worst excesses of racism. In 1906 black infantrymen in the 25th Regiment, stationed at Fort Brown, Texas, were attacked by local whites whenever they set foot in the nearby town of Brownsville. White racists made it clear that blacks were not welcome, beating up any who ventured into town, even threatening them with guns. One hot night, in the early-morning hours of August 14, African Americans fought back, leaving one white civilian dead. This event was splashed in headlines across the country, with editorials calling for the expulsion of men of color from the military.

Benjamin Davis Sr., one of the first black officers to rise through the ranks.

U.S. MILITARY HISTORY INSTITUTE

When military investigators could not determine which soldiers had been involved, officials threatened three companies of men with court-martial if they did not reveal the names of the guilty parties. Ultimately President Theodore Roosevelt took matters into his own hands: 160 black soldiers, including 6 Congressional Medal of Honor winners, received dishonorable discharges. Black leaders bitterly denounced Roosevelt's actions, which were ratified by Congress in 1908. It took more than half a century of protests to reverse this decision. Finally, in 1972, after nearly seventy years of petitions, the Secretary of the Army issued honorable discharges to those who were unfairly punished.

Black soldiers knew that the Brownsville affair was a sign of the times. The U.S. military was still not immune to prejudice and reflected the racial double standard that was part of the larger society.

In 1916, when Mexican rebel leader Pancho Villa led a raid into New Mexico, killing many Americans, President Woodrow Wilson responded by ordering General "Black Jack" Pershing to cross the Rio Grande into Mexico with five thousand troops.

During this campaign, Major Charles Young, at the head of the Tenth Cavalry, a black unit, distinguished himself in combat. He and his men performed bravely during an engagement in which they rescued a trapped white cavalry unit. In recognition of his outstanding leadership, Pershing had Young promoted to lieutenant colonel. But military skirmishes along the Mexican border were soon overshadowed by war in Europe.

NINE

World War I and After
1917–1940

✶ ✶ ✶ ✶ ✶ ✶ ✶ ✶ ✶ ✶ ✶ ✶ ✶

IRONICALLY IT WAS WARTIME that created the opportunity for accelerated advancement of black soldiers. The United States remained neutral in
1914, whereas the Allied nations of Britain, France, and Russia went to war
against the Central Powers of Germany and the Austro-Hungarian
Empire. President Woodrow Wilson campaigned in the presidential elec-
tion of 1916 to keep America out of the European war. However, events
overtook Wilson, and the United States entered World War I in April 1917.
Americans were primed for battle, and African Americans, as always, volunteered: more than seven hundred thousand black men lined up to enlist
on Registration Day, July 5, 1917.

In the face of this overwhelming show of black patriotism, the Selective
Service (the draft board) developed a quota system to limit the number of
African American volunteers. The military was willing to accept only one
black for every seven white recruits. Also, the draft stated: "White and colored enlisted or enrolled men shall not be organized in or assigned to the
same company, battalion, or regiment."

Thus when American men were sent to military camps to train for
World War I, the U.S. military again treated black recruits unfairly. Only a

African Americans in uniform during World War I. U.S. MILITARY HISTORY INSTITUTE

small percentage of black troops were offered combat training. And the army only reluctantly created a black officers' training school—at Camp Des Moines, Iowa.

Overall, more than 400,000 blacks enlisted, but only 42,000 were given an opportunity to fight. Of the 200,000 blacks sent to France, 160,000 were restricted to menial jobs such as working in the motor pool, loading and offloading goods at the docks, preparing meals, and so on. Dough-

Black soldiers in the trenches in Europe during World War I.
U.S. MILITARY HISTORY INSTITUTE

boys (American combat troops in World War I) would remain over-whelmingly white.

Charles Young, the West Point graduate who had distinguished himself in the Spanish-American War and in combat in Mexico, was eager for an overseas command after President Wilson declared war. Young was certainly deserving, and by all rights he should have been promoted and sent with black troops to France. But when the army declared him "unfit for service" for reasons of health, it was a slap in the face. Young wanted to disprove this charge, and so the fifty-three-year-old colonel rode on horseback from his Ohio home to Washington, D.C., to protest the army's decision.

Despite his feat, Young was retired from active service. Clearly the American military was unwilling to send black officers into command roles in combat. A white Southerner's persistent complaints about serving under Young and a Mississippi senator's letters to the War Department influenced the army's decision to retire Young.

That left only one other black officer available for combat assignment in Europe: First Lieutenant Benjamin Davis Sr. He and his black troops, the Ninth Cavalry, were stationed in the Philippines in 1917. All four of the regular army units filled with black troops—trained, veteran soldiers— were not posted to Europe for duty, but instead were sent to patrol the Mexican border or stationed in Hawaii or the Philippines. Trained and disciplined black soldiers were kept from the European theater of war.

Again, despite all these obstacles, some African American soldiers made it to Europe and seized any opportunity to defeat racist assumptions. The Fighting 369th Regiment was detached to the French command and performed spectacularly, despite having only brief and rudimentary military training. The 369th landed in France in 1918 and remained on the front lines for 191 consecutive days, earning the nickname "Hellfighters" from the Germans. These black soldiers were beloved for their military valor as well as renowned for their jazz band.

One of the great heroic incidents of the war involved two black sentries. On May 14, 1917, a party of thirty German soldiers surprised Privates Henry Johnson and Needham Roberts of the 369th. The two black soldiers fought off the enemy in hand-to-hand combat, wounding ten and killing four. This amazing feat became known as the Battle of Henry Johnson and was celebrated in verse and song. For their valor, Johnson and Roberts became the first Americans to receive the French croix de guerre.

Although the French greeted black soldiers warmly and offered them equal hospitality, American military commanders insisted that color lines be drawn and segregation enforced in accommodation and eating facilities. They also warned local Frenchwomen not to "fraternize" with black soldiers, thus creating a hostile climate for African Americans abroad.

Ten thousand American women were shipped to France with the Army Nursing Corps and the American Red Cross, but both groups prohibited the participation of black women. Less than a dozen black women were recruited through the Salvation Army, the Young Women's Christian Association (YWCA), and other networks for service abroad. A handful of women organized separate canteens (snack bars at military installations) for black soldiers, as white women banned African American doughboys from using theirs.

By Armistice Day, in November 1918, there were 750 dead and 5,000 wounded among the African American troops. Despite this sacrifice, black troops at Brest, France, were asked to load coal onto boats to send home white troops—they would have to wait for separate and unequal transportation home.

In only one instance were they accorded a hero's welcome: during a parade in New York City honoring Private Johnson and comrades of the 369th. The black veterans were cheered along their marching route from lower Manhattan, up Fifth Avenue, and all the way home to Harlem. Ever a champion of black troops, General "Black Jack" Pershing, commander of

Crowds line the streets of Manhattan as black soldiers marched up Fifth Avenue, home to Harlem. NATIONAL ARCHIVES

American forces in France, addressed the all-black 92d Division: "The American public has every reason to be proud of your record."

But it was a tough, bitter homecoming for most African American veterans. Although decorated by foreign governments for their bravery, no black American combat soldier was awarded a Medal of Honor. Many black soldiers came home feeling that their white officers had spent too

Private Henry Johnson in a victory parade in New York City. NATIONAL ARCHIVES

much time fighting them instead of the Germans. As the great black leader W. E. B. DuBois remarked, "With Armistice came disillusion."

DuBois sailed to France to obtain documentation of the military's systematic discrimination. In his investigations, DuBois discovered that there was no foundation to many of the charges whites had made about black soldiers. He found evidence that blacks had conducted themselves with dignity and valor; rarely were they the drunken, carousing stereotypes white critics had claimed. DuBois also went to the villages where white officers had complained that blacks stationed nearby had committed disgraceful crimes—rapes of local women. DuBois interviewed mayors and other officials, who denied such outrages.

After the war, renewed campaigns of white supremacy caused more problems. Members of the white brass (military command) discredited black soldiers. Major General W. H. Hay, the white commander of the 184th Infantry Brigade of the 92d Division, argued against having black officers and continually denigrated black soldiers. Hay believed that World War I had proved the "inherent weaknesses of the negro character, especially lack of intelligence and initiative." He further asserted that the black soldier would not follow a "negro officer into battle, no matter how good the officer may be, with the same confidence that he will follow a white man." He argued against training black officers and thought black soldiers should be kept out of combat and be restricted to labor battalions in future conflicts. These views contributed to an immediate decline in the number of blacks in the military.

In 1919 the standing army shrank to thirty thousand. African Americans were barred from the ranks unless they had already served. Furthermore, any blacks who enlisted were confined to the infantry and not given any opportunity for advancement. These and other injustices fueled racial tensions.

These tensions flared into flames, and in the summer of 1919, full-scale race riots erupted across the nation, with whites attacking blacks and blacks fighting back. During a ten-day stretch of violence in Chicago, thirty-eight people were killed and more than five hundred were wounded. In the same year, seventy-seven African Americans were murdered by white mobs. Those lynched included ten black veterans, some killed while still in uniform. The heroic deeds of black soldiers were all too quickly forgotten.

Even honoring those who died in combat would become a matter of racial conflict. Tablets listing the American war-dead often placed the names of black martyrs on separate plaques, enforcing Jim Crow even for those who had given their lives for their country.

The U.S. government sent boatloads of Gold Star Mothers (women who had lost sons during the war) to Europe to visit the graves of soldiers awarded medals. It was a painful indignity that black mothers were sent on separate ships. These insults created a backlash among African Americans and whites struggling for racial equality.

Blacks kept pushing for equal access to opportunity in the military. They enrolled in Reserve Officers Training Corps (ROTC) programs at black colleges like Wilberforce University (Ohio), Howard University (Washington, D.C.), and Tuskegee Institute (Alabama). A younger generation was determined to expand and build upon the achievements of black pioneers in the military.

One of the most outstanding of these young black men was Benjamin O. Davis Jr., son of Benjamin O. Davis Sr. The younger Davis was born in 1912 and was attending the University of Chicago when his congressman, Oscar S. DePriest, the only black in Congress, nominated him for West Point in 1932.

Davis Jr., like Henry Flipper sixty years before him, attended the Point and suffered in silence; he ate all his meals alone and roomed by himself for four long years. In 1936 Davis became the first black graduate of West Point in the twentieth century. Army officials then wanted to send him to law school, hoping they could eventually shuffle him off into the judge advocate's office.

Benjamin O. Davis Sr. and his son, Benjamin O. Davis Jr.

U.S. MILITARY HISTORY INSTITUTE

But Davis, like his father before him, refused the easy way out and insisted on a regular appointment. He was assigned to command a black company in Fort Benning, Georgia. When he arrived on base, white officers refused to speak to him except in the line of duty. The only other black officer at Fort Benning was his own father. Both father and son were excluded from the officers' club, but the Davises refused to bow in the face of these indignities.

Soon after, James Lee Johnson Jr. was admitted to the Naval Academy, the first black to attend Annapolis in over sixty years. In less than a year Johnson, along with more than a hundred classmates, was let go because of "academic inadequacy." Black cadets, though, would continue to struggle against the color line.

These were dispiriting times for blacks in the military, as African Americans constituted less than 2 percent of the combined regular army and National Guard units. Black men in the navy felt at an equal disadvantage. In 1940 thirteen black sailors sent a letter to the *Pittsburgh Courier,* a black newspaper, describing their menial duty assignments and complaining that they were restricted to serving as "bellhops, chambermaids, and dishwashers." The navy responded by discharging all those who had signed their names to this letter of protest, and proclaimed, "The policy of not enlisting men of the colored race for any branch of the naval service except the messman's branch was adopted to meet the best interests of the general ship efficiency." (This position was endorsed by Secretary of the Navy Frank Knox, the same Frank Knox who had praised black soldiers' bravery in battle when he served with them during the Spanish-American War.)

The maltreatment of black soldiers stationed in the South remained particularly problematic. Brawls and gunfire erupted too frequently. M.P.s (Military Police) allowed local authorities to handle disturbances between servicemen and townspeople when it involved racial conflicts. The military was all too eager to downplay racial incidents, even murder. In 1941 Private Felix Hall, a black soldier, was found hanging from a tree near Fort Benning, Georgia, with his hands tied behind his back—clearly the victim of a lynching. Authorities labeled his death a suicide. By then both Benjamin O. Davis Sr. and his son had left Fort Benning and had been posted to other assignments. Davis Sr. was assigned to the 369th Infantry, which now was part of New York State's National Guard. In 1940 he became the first black general in the U.S. Army. His son was in charge of ROTC training at Tuskegee Institute, a primarily black college in Alabama. As military men, they were not allowed to challenge the authorities but welcomed support from civilian quarters.

Black leaders spoke out against peacetime injustices in the military. They agitated for reform with President Franklin Delano Roosevelt, elected in 1932 and reelected in 1936.

In 1940 Roosevelt approved new draft regulations that read: "There shall be no discrimination against any person on account of race or color." Roosevelt was perhaps influenced by his wife Eleanor's well-known commitment to fair and equal treatment for African Americans. The government agreed to raise the quota for blacks in the military to 9 percent—equivalent to their ratio in the population. Perhaps because war had broken out in Europe again in 1939, leaders in the United States recognized that they soon might have to mobilize black soldiers in yet another foreign war.

TEN

World War II
1941–1945

★ ★ ★ ★ ★ ★ ★ ★ ★ ★ ★ ★ ★

WHEN THE JAPANESE BOMBED Pearl Harbor on Sunday, December 7, 1941, Dorie Miller, a black mess cook aboard the U.S.S. *Arizona,* rushed on deck and saw his captain wounded on the bridge. At great personal risk, Miller carried his commander to safety. Next he grabbed a machine gun and shot down at least two and perhaps as many as four Japanese planes. After great pressure from black leaders and civil rights groups, this fearless sailor, the son of Texan sharecroppers, won the Navy Cross for his brave actions. Miller was never promoted from the ranks of mess duty, despite his proven talents. When a Japanese submarine in the South Pacific torpedoed his ship in 1944, Miller was lost at sea.

After Pearl Harbor, Roosevelt officially declared war, joining the Allied powers (England, France, and Russia) against the Axis powers (Germany, Japan, and Italy). At the time, there were only two black officers in the army: General Benjamin O. Davis Sr. and his son, Captain Benjamin O. Davis Jr.

Long before Pearl Harbor, during the military crisis in Europe, one young black man, Yancy Williams, had pressured the U.S. military to open a pilot's training school for blacks. In 1940, the Army Flying School

Black pilots in training (Benjamin O. Davis Jr. third from left).
U.S. MILITARY HISTORY INSTITUTE

in Alabama, which became the home of renowned military pilots, the Tuskegee Airmen, opened its doors. The ambitious Davis Jr. completed his flight training at Tuskegee and was assigned to lead the first black unit of the Army Air Force, the 99th Pursuit Squadron. After his promotion first to major and then to lieutenant colonel, Davis took his pilots to

North Africa, where the squadron, known as the Black Eagles, flew combat missions in Africa, Sicily, and Italy, never losing a single Allied bomber to enemy planes. During World War II, graduates of the Tuskegee program flew more than fifteen thousand bombing and escort missions, shooting down 136 enemy aircraft and destroying 273 planes on the ground.

Military necessity in World War II dramatically accelerated the expansion of roles for blacks in the military. The overwhelming majority of military enlistees were in the army, but gains were made in other branches of the service as well. The number of black sailors grew from 4,000 in 1941 to more than 160,000 by 1945. Six hundred African Americans were trained as pilots for the air force, with 450 coming out of Tuskegee.

More than 17,000 blacks joined the U.S. Marines, which had long remained an all-white preserve. If an African American could survive marine boot camp—the harshest training in the military—he was considered fit to serve with this exclusive warrior elite. The marines were the first branch of the military not to assign blacks to separate units, so black "leathernecks" (as marines were nicknamed) were fully integrated into the entry-level ranks, where they remained throughout the war.

Only one other branch of the war effort was more progressive, the civilian-operated merchant marine, which was fully integrated: blacks and whites shared eating and sleeping facilities. Also, blacks were promoted to officer status. Unfortunately, the military brass continued to resist this model.

Black women too broke the color barrier for the first time, joining the women's branches of the armed forces: 4,000 WACs (Women's Army

Black women served in uniform in large numbers for the first time in World War II.
U.S. MILITARY HISTORY INSTITUTE

Corps) in the army and 60 WAVES (Women Accepted for Volunteer Emergency Service) in the navy. The navy enlisted many fewer women because women did shore duty to release men for duty aboard ship, but black men's service assignments at sea were still not considered a top military priority.

Altogether one million black men and women served in the American military during World War II; eventually three out of four black soldiers

General Benjamin O. Davis Sr. (the first black soldier to reach this rank) reviewing the troops during World War II. U.S. MILITARY HISTORY INSTITUTE

served overseas. Despite these impressive gains, only six blacks joined Davis Jr. at the rank of colonel, and his father remained the only African American to hold the rank of general throughout World War II.

Discrimination at every level continued to rankle African Americans in the military, especially on the home front. Before the war the American Red Cross had even refused to allow African Americans to donate blood. The head of the Red Cross conceded that there was no biological basis for believing "black blood" was different from "white blood" but bowed to racist attitudes. During wartime, African Americans were allowed to donate blood, but their blood was stored separately; blood supplies were collected and distributed on a segregated basis until 1963.

Black nurses were frequently assigned to prisoner-of-war camps. They were allowed to treat only captives or black soldiers, never white officers. In addition, white nurses were provided with housekeeping services, but black ones were expected to clean their own showers and latrines. Further, many black nurses stationed in outposts like Fort Huachuca, Arizona, resented going into town and discovering that they were barred from local restaurants. To add insult to injury, most of these segregated establishments were willing to serve enemy prisoners.

In March 1945 the *Crisis,* the journal of the National Association for the Advancement of Colored People (NAACP), edited by W. E. B. DuBois, reported: "Nothing so lowers Negro morale as the frequent preferential treatment of the Axis [German or Italian] prisoners of war in contrast with deprecating Army policy toward American troops who happen to be Negro."

Race leaders tried to emphasize that equal treatment was a patriotic necessity. Military recruiters, for their part, complained that many African Americans, aware of the "democratic malpractices accorded our men and women in the army," did not rush to enlist. Thus, segregation interfered with effective military recruitment.

William Hastie, a black civilian adviser to the War Department, reported to Assistant Secretary of War John J. McCloy, who was in charge of the question of "Negro troops." Despite Hastie's arguments in favor of integration, McCloy remained indifferent, ignoring evidence of discrimination and even violence against black troops. In January 1943, after months of witnessing McCloy turn a deaf ear to his pleas, Hastie resigned so that he could publicly express his disappointment with government policy.

Black troops sent to England in the summer of 1942 were allowed to play only supportive roles for white troops sent into combat. The army wanted to maintain segregated practices and to keep black soldiers in inferior roles. U.S. military brass requested that their British hosts help them maintain Jim Crow, but the English resisted.

In September 1942, the British Home Office refused to enforce regulations for segregation, and welcomed all American troops, regardless of color, to social events for soldiers. U.S. Army officials then tried to keep black and white troops apart by issuing passes (permission to go off base) on alternate days—adopting an odd-even pass system to keep blacks and whites from fraternizing on their days off. They also posted a list of establishments for whites only, and in some cases certain towns and villages were declared off limits for blacks. Officials used the military police to enforce segregation policies.

Conditions in the navy remained deplorable as well. More than 40 percent of black sailors in wartime service were assigned to menial roles on shipboard, as cooks, waiters, and valets. The rest were restricted to roles as stevedores (loading and offloading goods at the docks) or as mechanics (assigned to ship maintenance). Of the more than 160,000 enlisted, only a small group of 1,000 were offered training in other areas. Further, black sailors complained that they were not given the same shore leave privileges as their white counterparts.

Despite protests, declining morale, and a lack of commitment to fair and

Black soldiers training stateside before being shipped abroad.

U.S. MILITARY HISTORY INSTITUTE

equal treatment, the military continued to enlist black volunteers. By early 1944, rising protests at home had caused the government to review its policy. McCloy finally changed his mind and on March 2, 1944, issued a strongly worded statement, arguing that "colored units should be introduced in combat at the earliest practical moment . . . we must . . . be more affirmative about the use of our negro troops." McCloy demanded that military commanders immediately implement plans for an integrated fighting force.

The marines responded well to this directive, and the air force bowed to the pressure; in both groups the percentage of enlisted African Americans had been particularly small. Although Secretary of War Henry Stimson advised, for purposes of morale, that black ground troops be sent into combat zones, many army officials made only halfhearted efforts. Nevertheless, some black troops sent abroad were at long last allowed to fight and served their country as warriors.

Once they made it to the front lines, there were still obstacles to overcome. Second Lieutenant Joseph Hairston recalled that his 92d Division was placed under the command of General Edward Almond, a white Virginian and graduate of the Virginia Military Institute. Unfortunately Almond was unable to hide his racist views from the men he commanded. The 92d suffered during its training in Arizona and later, while stationed in Europe. When Hairston and his fellow soldiers were deployed to Italy in October 1944, Almond ordered a regiment to the front lines, but without bullets for their weapons, as he did not "trust" colored troops with live ammunition! Hairston recalled it was a terrible ordeal to try to endure such hostile treatment.

Eventually the men got their ammunition, but they were given little guidance and therefore performed poorly. They also had to fight bad press, as both white officers and reporters questioned their abilities. During the heat of battle, it was rumored that members of the 92d Division "melted away" in the face of enemy attack and this slander against the division shattered the men's morale. (A 1992 independent study of their conduct resulted in different findings, and two soldiers in Hairston's unit were nominated for the Medal of Honor.)

Even black soldiers who had performed valiantly in combat, such as African American marines serving in the Pacific theater, found themselves subjected to a double standard when off duty. In one case black leather-necks who had helped the Allies conquer Guam were stationed on the island during the fall of 1944. A tense atmosphere developed between black and white troops. Taunts and scuffles erupted into a full-scale riot in December 1944, with military police injured trying to calm an angry mob.

But despite the extreme prejudice to which they were exposed, black soldiers in Europe and in the Pacific distinguished themselves. Sergeant Jerry Davis won the Legion of Merit after being pinned down during the Battle of Pisa in Italy for more than ten hours. He was wounded while crossing an open field, trying to rescue members of his unit. Davis was the first black soldier in World War II to be so honored. Private Isaac Sermon was a black hero in the South Pacific, where he won the Silver Star. He was wounded four times while using his Browning automatic to return enemy fire in nose-to-nose combat in the Solomon Islands.

Commanders reluctant to use black troops in battle often were forced to use the human resources at hand despite their prejudices. In November

Black and white soldiers together honoring their fallen comrades in World War II.
U.S. MILITARY HISTORY INSTITUTE

1944 the infamous George S. Patton welcomed the all-black 761st Tank Battalion into his campaign with the greeting: "I don't care what color you are as long as you go up there and kill those Kraut sons of bitches!" The 761st performed courageously, earning a dozen Silver Stars, more than 60 Bronze Stars, and 280 Purple Hearts.

Indeed, by war's end, manpower shortages necessitated the integration of white divisions with black battalions to keep up troop strength. This created large numbers of "mixed units." Many white officers in charge of these units reported that integration proved a great success. Military brass, nevertheless, resisted changing army policy, claiming, "The Army is not an instrument of social reform."

With the German defeat in May 1945, followed by the Japanese surrender in September 1945, the Allies celebrated a hard-won victory. Black troops as well as white soldiers, black women in uniform as well as white, could take pride in their role in defeating the enemy.

ELEVEN

Battles on the Home Front 1946–1950

✶ ✶ ✶ ✶ ✶ ✶ ✶ ✶ ✶ ✶ ✶ ✶

ALTHOUGH VICTORY WAS WRESTED from enemies abroad, African American servicemen and women wondered whether racism in the military could ever be defeated. In 1946 Robert Powell was shipped home with his Silver Star but found that little had changed: "A soldier was looked on as a hero if he had medals on his chest but still it was the back of the bus for us."

When no black soldiers were awarded the Congressional Medal of Honor, Congresswoman Helen Gahagan Douglas complained on Capitol Hill that the black soldier "fought and shed his blood for a freedom that he has not been permitted fully to share." It would take nearly forty years and several congressional investigations for black candidates for the Medal of Honor to be recommended for their World War II heroism.

In June 1941 Franklin Roosevelt had issued an executive order that forbade discrimination on the basis of color in hiring in defense industries. He tried to guarantee enforcement by creating the Fair Employment Practices Committee to supervise defense plants. More than a million blacks left the South to find jobs in northern war industries. By 1945, almost two million African Americans were employed in war plants throughout the country.

Harry S. Truman honors Benjamin O. Davis Sr. upon his retirement, and is the first President to call for an end to segregation in the U.S. armed forces.
U.S. MILITARY HISTORY INSTITUTE

But when the war ended, many of these industries restored the color line. Black soldiers who had hoped to translate their skills into peacetime jobs were disappointed. Upon his return home, former pilot Roscoe Brown, who had flown with the 332d Fighter Group, applied to Eastern Airlines for a flying job. The man behind the desk threw his application in the trash, saying, "We don't hire colored."

After World War II, African Americans were denied their fair share of government benefits for veterans—housing, tuition, job training, and other assistance offered by Congress' GI Bill. Angry blacks demanded change and decided not to give up the fight. Race leaders focused on obtaining fair treatment for black soldiers—as a key step to ensure black equality for all Americans.

With an open enlistment policy in peacetime, white military leaders feared that African Americans would flood into the army. So they limited the number of blacks allowed to enlist and required that black volunteers score thirty points higher than the minimum score required for whites. This policy demonstrated the military's continuing commitment to racial discrimination.

President Harry S. Truman, who had been sworn into office when Franklin Roosevelt died in April 1945, became concerned about the complaints of black veterans following a 1946 incident. Sergeant Isaac Woodward, on furlough after fifteen months' service in the South Pacific, was heading home from Georgia. Along the way, Woodward was accused of disorderly conduct by a bus driver, taken off the bus by a local sheriff, and beaten while in police custody. When Woodward was finally admitted to an army hospital, damage to his eye had caused permanent blindness. The sheriff was later acquitted of any crime. Truman publicly commented on the case: "When a Mayor and a City Marshal can take a negro Sergeant off a bus in South Carolina, beat him up and put out one of his eyes and nothing is done about it by the State Authorities, something is radically wrong with the system."

When Davis Sr. retired from the army, he denounced segregation:

"There is no such animal as separate but equal." African Americans had heeded their country in time of need, and black leadership believed they could no longer be expected to fight for the democracy of others abroad while being denied their own freedoms at home.

On July 26, 1948, Truman took a bold and unpopular step by issuing a strongly worded executive order: "It is the declared policy of the President that there shall be equality of treatment and opportunity for all persons in the Armed Services without regard to race, color, or national origins."

Truman's directive reflected and pioneered a massive civil rights movement in the United States. The desegregation of the American military was a great tribute to generations of black soldiers who had come before, and an important boost for the African American men and women in the military who would follow.

TWELVE

Korea
1950–1953

★ ★ ★ ★ ★ ★ ★ ★ ★ ★ ★ ★ ★

IN JUNE 1950, WHEN NORTH KOREANS invaded South Korea, the United States became involved in a three-year-long war to drive back "Communist aggression." President Truman named General Douglas MacArthur as supreme commander of the force to be sent to Korea by the newly formed United Nations. And the United States assigned blacks to serve in combat units side by side with whites. Even more radical, for the first time, black officers were placed in command of whites. This was a revolutionary transformation.

Some branches of the military had responded more swiftly than others to Truman's 1948 desegregation directive. The U.S. Air Force pushed for full integration, whereas the army command dragged its feet. The navy claimed it had already integrated, but critics felt they had a long way to go.

Truman had initially sent troops to Korea as part of a "police action," to avoid obtaining a declaration of war from Congress. Therefore many Korea-bound U.S. troops, black and white, thought their job would be to back the South Korean army. But they soon found themselves on the front lines, engaged in fierce encounters with a well-equipped enemy. Although MacArthur had promised his troops that they would be "home

Black and white sailors serve together, shelling enemy strongholds during the Korean War. NATIONAL ARCHIVES

by Christmas," it became apparent that the fight would be a longer, more difficult haul.

Everett Copeland was a black veteran of World War II who had served with the 92d Division. As a reservist, he was called up by the army in July 1950, and sent to Korea after only thirty days' training. Many months later, he found himself on patrol in the eastern mountains of Korea, ill prepared and ill equipped. Copeland complained that not only was his unit without

Operations in the field could be harsh and grueling during the Korean War.
U.S. MILITARY HISTORY INSTITUTE

proper winter clothing, but the soldiers couldn't build fires for warmth for fear of alerting the enemy to their position.

For two to three weeks, Copeland's unit stumbled across bodies of frozen soldiers, men killed by the cold. Copeland also discovered that their North Korean opponents were only too willing to employ brutal tactics as the battles dragged on. He described with chilling horror: "The enemy would drive captive groups of civilians before him, groups of women, chil-

African American soldiers served in Korea in larger proportion than in any other previous war. U.S. MILITARY HISTORY INSTITUTE

dren and elderly. They were driven straight into our mine fields to blow a path with their bodies right up to our barbwire fences."

Despite its horrors, combat experience offered blacks opportunities for advancement. The Marine Corps had taken seriously Truman's demand to provide equal treatment for black recruits. When the Korean War began, 427 of the 1,500 African Americans in the marines were confined to the role of steward. By war's end, there were another 100 stewards, but there were also nearly 15,000 black marines. This remarkable transition took place smoothly over the three-year war. African American leathernecks made great strides, seizing the opportunity for combat duty and glory. Rifleman A. C. Clark, a black marine, received two decorations: first a Bronze Star for rescuing his platoon leader while under fire, then a Silver Star for killing three enemy, taking out a machine gun, and covering the evacuation of wounded men while he himself was shot twice.

Two black soldiers, Private William Thompson and Sergeant Cornelius Charlton, received America's highest honor and were posthumously (after their deaths) awarded the Congressional Medal of Honor.

The war in Korea required a lot of air power and gave black pilots a chance to serve in larger numbers than ever before. Benjamin O. Davis Jr. arrived in Korea to command a mixed unit of black and white fliers. World War II veteran pilot Daniel "Chappie" James showed great courage during his many combat flights over Korea. In one particularly intense mission, he was credited with eliminating more than one hundred enemy. After flying his tour of one hundred missions, he was returned to the United States, having earned the Distinguished Flying Cross.

In 1948 Jessie L. Brown became the first black naval aviator. He was awarded the Distinguished Flying Cross in 1950 for his courage in strafing the enemy (providing air cover for troops on the ground) to protect marines in battles. The award was presented posthumously, as he died in the line of duty. In 1973 the navy named a ship after him, a destroyer escort, and he became the first African American to be so honored.

Despite honor and advancement, intolerance and resentment continued. White racists resisted the military's policy of integration. When white sol-

A navy poster honoring the black naval aviator who won the Distinguished Flying Cross and died in combat. A ship was named in his honor.

U.S. NAVAL HISTORICAL CENTER

diers hurled racial slurs and insults at black comrades in the field, too many white commanders ignored them. Black attorney Thurgood Marshall, touring in Korea on behalf of the NAACP, discovered that black soldiers were disproportionately charged with desertion, often being convicted on trumped-up charges. His investigation confirmed that court-martials of black soldiers were not being handled fairly.

African American combat troops posing in their jeep in Korea.
U.S. MILITARY HISTORY INSTITUTE

Also, many men discovered that camaraderie across the color line while in the trenches might not mean better race relations during peacetime. While sailing home, Copeland greeted a white soldier whom he had carried injured off the field. When the white soldier, who was playing cards on deck, ignored him, Copeland reminded him of their encounter in battle, but the soldier dismissed him, saying, "I know who you are, boy."

The integrated combat force during the Korean War increased debates at home about America's military role abroad. After the 1953 truce, the majority of black soldiers returned from Korea to confront a society ripe for social change. Black leaders continued their crusade for justice and equality, and they would soon be joined by larger and larger numbers of white allies. The following year, in 1954, the Supreme Court struck down the policy of "separate but equal" with its *Brown v. Board of Education* ruling, thus providing for the desegregation of public schools, which paved the way for the modern civil rights movement.

THIRTEEN

Vietnam
1965–1975

★ ★ ★ ★ ★ ★ ★ ★ ★ ★ ★ ★ ★

BY 1965, AFRICAN AMERICANS made up roughly 10 percent of the American population. Military service seemed a better alternative to the high rates of unemployment that many young black men faced, and the black soldier was well represented in all branches of the military: 15 percent of the army, 5 percent of the navy, 9 percent of the marines, and 8 percent of the air force. With their increasing numbers in the military and their integration into combat roles, African Americans would pay an even higher price during America's next major military offensive, the Vietnam War.

In the early 1960s, once again the United States entered a war abroad "to prevent the spread of Communism," this time becoming involved with the European conflict in Indochina. The United States offered support to the South Vietnamese in their war against North Vietnam, a nation assisted by Communist allies.

By 1965, there were 100,000 integrated American troops in Vietnam. By the spring of 1966, nearly 4,000 dead had been shipped home in body bags. By 1967, nearly half a million American troops were stationed in Vietnam. Initially, during the Kennedy administration (1961–1963), Amer-

Black soldiers stand guard during an unloading operation at Quinhon.
U.S. MILITARY HISTORY INSTITUTE

ican soldiers served as "military advisers" helping to train South Vietnamese troops. But the numbers of U.S. servicemen sent abroad grew under the presidency of Lyndon Baines Johnson (1963–1969), and the nature of their mission changed radically, as they were coerced into combat operations. American infantrymen started serving on the front lines in this complex and dangerous conflict.

An African American seaman loads his M-16 rifle, as he stands watch.

NATIONAL ARCHIVES

Black soldiers were drawn into the infantry ranks in larger and larger numbers. Young black men were drafted at rates double those of young white men: in 1968 the number of eligible African Americans drafted was 64 percent, whereas the white rate was 31 percent. Since fewer than 2 percent of those serving on draft boards were black (and there were no African Americans on selective service committees in Deep South states like Alabama, Louisiana, and Mississippi), these higher rates of blacks in the army could be interpreted as a direct result of racial discrimination. Young white men were given improved chances for deferment, while blacks were disproportionately required to serve. Rev. Martin Luther King Jr. spoke for many when he asserted: "We have been faced with the cruel irony of watching Negro and white boys on TV screens as they kill and die together for a nation that has been unable to seat them together in the same schools."

This criticism was powerfully brought home in 1967 when Muhammad Ali, perhaps the most famous African American of his day and one of the best-known black men in the world (winner of the 1960 Olympic gold medal for boxing and the 1964 World Heavyweight title), refused induction into the U.S. Army. When he was drafted, Ali declined to serve, citing his religious beliefs as a member of the Nation of Islam. But he also proclaimed: "My enemy is the white people, not Viet Cong or Chinese or Japanese. You're my foes when I want freedom, you're my foes when I want justice. You're my foes when I want equality."

As a result, Ali was stripped of his boxing title, charged with draft evasion, and found guilty. He appealed the ruling, and in 1971 the U.S. Supreme Court overturned his conviction. Ali's criticism of the Vietnam War and his argument that racism at home was the real enemy of black Americans heightened the controversy over U.S. involvement in Southeast Asia.

While a good number of African Americans took Ali's advice to heart, protesting the war or fleeing to Canada to avoid induction (becoming "draft dodgers"), many more blacks served loyally in Vietnam. During the first few years of the war, the number of blacks who died in Vietnam rose to nearly 25 percent of the total. This shocking rate was almost double their ratio in the ranks. Because of adverse publicity, by 1968 the government sought ways to rotate blacks out of combat tours of duty, a policy that substantially reduced fatalities among African American servicemen.

Black servicemen in Vietnam were more concerned with survival than military policy. Many believed what one infantryman argued: "We're all soldiers. The only color we know is khaki and green. The color of mud and the color of the blood is all the same." Black platoon leader Joe Anderson commanded a well-integrated unit in Vietnam, where he believed "race was never an issue. You didn't worry about color; you only wanted someone to cover your back."

Second Lieutenant Anderson was on his first assignment "in country" (the interior of Vietnam), sent out to rescue a missing platoon, when he and his men were attacked by enemy forces and were outnumbered ten to one. Anderson's unit fought through the night, and by daybreak the Vietcong had retreated. Anderson was able to locate survivors and bring his men back to safety. For his valor, he was awarded the Silver Star, won during his first time under fire.

African Americans, in this war as in others, performed their share of heroic deeds. But during the Vietnam War many more black soldiers were

During the Vietnam War, African Americans began to receive medals, promotions, and awards in larger numbers, which reflected their military accomplishments.
U.S. MILITARY HISTORY INSTITUTE

rewarded for their valor than in previous foreign wars. Private Milton Olive of the 173d Airborne Brigade, already a recipient of the Purple Heart for courage under fire, threw himself on a live grenade to save the men in his company at Phy Cuong. Private Olive was only nineteen when he died. This earned him the posthumously awarded Congressional Medal of Honor in 1966; he was one of twenty blacks to receive America's highest military decoration during the Vietnam War.

By war's end, America had spent $150 billion of its resources on military campaigns in Southeast Asia. More than fifty-eight thousand young Americans had lost their lives during this war. Leaders like Martin Luther King Jr. opposed this steep sacrifice, warning: "The promises of the Great Society have been shot down on the battlefield of Vietnam."

By the time the peace accords were signed between North and South Vietnam in 1973, ending American military involvement, protest and reform movements in the United States were reshaping social conditions at home. The antiwar movement and black resentment over the burdens the war had imposed transformed America's role in Vietnam, forcing an end to the conflict. Back home, black Americans wanted the government—and the military—to make good on promises of equality and were willing to fight for what was right.

FOURTEEN

Fighting for Freedom 1954–1990

✯ ✯ ✯ ✯ ✯ ✯ ✯ ✯ ✯ ✯ ✯ ✯

WHEN THE SUPREME COURT launched its attack on segregation with the 1954 *Brown v. Board of Education* decision, African Americans renewed their challenge to southern systems of discrimination: they went on the front lines of protest and created a movement of foot soldiers for freedom. The Montgomery Bus Boycott, launched in December 1955, brought Martin Luther King Jr. and the Southern Christian Leadership Conference into the national limelight. Blacks demanded support from the federal government on this important issue of desegregation.

In September 1957 the governor of Arkansas refused to send troops to quell rioting white students in Little Rock who chanted "Two, four, six, eight: we ain't gonna integrate." President Dwight Eisenhower federalized the National Guard and sent in one thousand troops from the 101st Airborne to restore order. This demonstrated that the federal government was willing to use its military might to protect blacks' rights. For the first time since the Civil War, American soldiers were on their own front lines, enforcing government reforms for racial equality.

In February 1960 black college students, tired of broken promises and postponed justice, staged sit-ins at segregated lunch counters in Greens-

National Guardsmen at Little Rock High School. CORBIS/BETTMANN-UPI

boro, North Carolina—peaceful protests against racially discriminatory laws. When they were arrested for breaking the law, many sang "We Shall Overcome" while being hauled off to jail. These new regiments of non-violent protesters were met with increasingly angry responses from whites infuriated by black resistance to segregation. Thousands of African Americans were joined by sympathetic whites in civil rights activities: voter registration drives, "freedom rides" (integrated buses traveling through the segregated South), and rallies and marches.

Although King preached a message of hope in his "I Have a Dream" speech during the march on Washington, D.C., in August 1963, a little

Martin Luther King Jr. was a strong voice of protest against the black soldiers' sacrifice without freedom and equality in their own country. CORBIS/BETTMANN-UPI

over two weeks later, four young black girls lost their lives in the bombing of a church in Birmingham, Alabama, a crime that shocked the nation. Black protests continued despite the violence. "Freedom fighters" were on the front lines, facing attacks by police with billy clubs, dogs, and powerful water hoses during their peaceful demonstrations. Many Americans watched in horror as scenes of police brutality and violence against young people were beamed into their living rooms on the nightly news.

In 1964 Malcolm X, a former leader within the Nation of Islam (Black Muslims), formed the Organization of Afro-American Unity to promote black nationalism. An advocate of black separatism and black pride, his radical philosophy challenged the politics of compromise promoted by more moderate black leaders. Until his assassination in 1965, he was a powerful voice for black militants, and after his death many of his ideas lived on within movements such as the Black Panthers.

With the growth of black-power movements and continuing pressure from activists for equality of opportunity, Congress at long last responded. One Senator commented: "No army can withstand the strength of an idea whose time has come." First, the Civil Rights Act of 1964 prohibited discrimination in voting, education, and hiring, as well as providing equal access to hotels, restaurants, buses, and other public facilities. Then in 1965 Congress approved the Voting Rights Act, which eliminated all literacy tests, prohibited poll taxes, and expanded federal powers to protect voters' rights. Despite these important pieces of federal legislation, many blacks wanted more and were impatient for change. The assassination of Martin Luther King Jr. in 1968 and the subsequent riots sweeping across the nation created waves of unrest.

Despite various setbacks, continuing protests in the 1960s and 1970s led to greater opportunities for blacks in the military. Many African Americans who had been waiting in the wings were now able to move into the spotlight in an equal opportunity army looking for black leadership. Daniel "Chappie" James Jr. had followed his mother's "eleventh commandment": "Thou shalt never quit." During World War II, James had risked his military career by protesting segregation, but he became a career military man and went on to brilliant achievement. During the Korean War, he won a Distinguished Flying Cross. And in Vietnam, James rapidly advanced and became an outstanding wing commander. In 1975 he was promoted to a four-star general and served as the commander of the prestigious North American Defense Command (NORAD) until his death in 1978.

Colin Powell, another rising star in the modern integrated army, was the Harlem-born son of Jamaican immigrants. Powell joined the Reserve Officers Training Corps (ROTC) while attending the City College of New York. After joining the army, Powell was posted to Fort Benning, Georgia, where he fought white racism and distinguished himself. Powell was offered a role as a military adviser in Vietnam. During his tour of duty in Southeast Asia, he began his dramatic climb up the military ladder.

Other achievements by African Americans in the military during this era include the following:

★ In 1967 Major Robert H. Lawrence Jr. of the U.S. Air Force was one of four pilots chosen for space flights. Although he was killed before he could serve, Lawrence was slated to become America's first black astronaut.

★ In 1971 Samuel Gravely became the first African American admiral in the U.S. Navy.

Admiral Samuel Gravely was a pioneer in the U.S. Navy, achieving his rank in 1971. U.S. NAVAL HISTORICAL CENTER

★ In 1972 Major General Frederick A. Davidson was named commanding general of the 8th Infantry Division in Europe, the first African American appointed to head an army division.

★ In June 1976 black women enrolled in the U.S. Naval Academy, and in 1980 Jamie Mines became the first African American woman to graduate.

★ In 1978 Frank E. Petersen Jr. became the first black general in the Marine Corps.

★ In 1978 Second Lieutenant Marcella Hayes earned her aviator wings in the U.S. Army, becoming the first black woman military pilot.

★ In 1978 Major Frederick Gregory and Major Guion S. Bluford joined Dr. Ronald McNair as pioneering African American astronaut trainees in the Space Aviation Program.

★ In 1979 Hazel W. Johnson was the first black woman general. In 1980 she became chief of the Army Nursing Corps.

During the 1970s, the military enforced policies that guaranteed greater opportunity for both black men and women. In 1972 there were three black West Point graduates, but in 1973 this number had jumped dramatically to more than twenty. And by the late 1980s the U.S. Military Academy at West Point graduated nearly fifty blacks per class, a trend that has since continued. Similar advancements were achieved at the U.S. Naval Academy in Maryland, the U.S. Air Force Academy in Colorado, and the U.S. Coast Guard Academy in Connecticut, where both young black men and black women have made great strides.

In 1970, when Admiral Elmo Zumwalt Jr., chief of naval operations, concluded, "There is no black navy, no white navy, just one navy—the

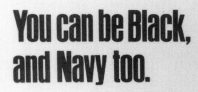

During the early 1970s the armed services projected a new attitude and actively recruited African Americans—as this navy poster indicates.

U.S. NAVAL HISTORICAL CENTER

United States Navy," he articulated the hopes of many commanders in the modern armed services.

Clearly the civil rights movement on the home front and African American military valor in wars abroad had combined to create a climate for permanent change in the 1980s, a change that would result in recognition for black military achievement and permanent improvements for African Americans in the armed services.

In 1988 General Colin Powell was promoted and became one of only ten four-star generals (and the only black one) in the U.S. Army. In 1989 President George Bush appointed Powell chairman of the Joint Chiefs of Staff, the first African American to assume such a high-ranking military post.

FIFTEEN

The Gulf War and Its Legacy 1991–1999

★ ★ ★ ★ ★ ★ ★ ★ ★ ★ ★ ★ ★

WHEN IRAQ INVADED KUWAIT in August 1990, American forces rushed to protect their Arab allies. At first the United Nations and other organizations attempted peaceful negotiations with Iraqi president Saddam Hussein, but eventually Arab leaders and their Western allies acknowledged that military force would be necessary to settle differences.

In the wake of this failed diplomacy, the United States sent more than half a million troops to the Gulf during the so-called Operation Desert Shield. Black and white pilots from the 101st Airborne Division flew their Apache helicopters deep into Iraqi territory on the early morning of January 17, 1991, as Operation Desert Shield shifted into Operation Desert Storm. The United States had begun its active participation in the Persian Gulf War. Not since World War II had such a massive air campaign been planned.

Air power played a significant role in determining the outcome of this war. Air attacks on Iraqi positions and expeditionary and amphibious forces initiated what was to become the first "high-tech war" in American

Black and white soldiers in tank units during the Gulf War.
U.S. MILITARY HISTORY INSTITUTE

history. Bombing and other operations were covered by the news media, with live audio reports and sometimes live televised images of battles.

Military operations included the first combat use of MRLs (multiple rocket launchers), artillery-spotting radar, and the "steel rain" of the DPICMs—large shells filled with small bomblets that rained down on a wide area.

American military operations included the use of Special Forces known as the Green Berets, who often traveled in large armored vehicles called Hummers, which were able to traverse rough and desert terrain. Hummers were equipped with grenade launchers and antitank-guided missiles. Some of the Green Berets on the front lines used hand-held designators to signal laser-guided smart bombs to blow up bridges and other important targets.

By February 16, American ground forces had launched intensive assaults, heavily shelling Iraqi lines to convince the enemy that they would not be deterred from their goal of pushing the invaders out of Kuwait. They were not afraid of the enemy's superior number of tanks; only the fear of chemical weapons kept American troops cautious.

Back home the anxious families of U.S. soldiers watched as broadcasters captured dramatic live images of the war. Some soldiers were able to use GPS (Global Positioning Satellite) technology to keep in touch with their loved ones halfway around the world.

The American public also watched as Colin Powell briefed the press on the war as events unfolded. Powell and General Norman Schwarzkopf (in charge of all the troops in the region) became the two most visible members of President George Bush's military team. For the first time in the nation's history, average Americans witnessed an African American military commander in a position of power and authority. Powell and Schwarzkopf exemplified the first fully integrated American military high command.

The Gulf War was remarkable in other ways too. Since the end of the military draft in 1973, all branches of the armed forces were voluntary. As a result, the ratio of African Americans in the modern military was higher

Chairman of the Joint Chiefs of Staff, General Colin Powell, the first African American to achieve such a high ranking and prestigious military position.

LIBRARY OF CONGRESS

than in the general population, as many young blacks found role models in the military. It was there that blacks sought the equality of opportunity they felt they could not find elsewhere. Although blacks constituted only 12 percent of those eligible for military service, more than 25 percent of the troops in the Gulf were black. Some have estimated that one in three soldiers in the combat arena was African American. When questioned about this ratio, Powell pragmatically responded: "There [i]s only one way to reduce the proportion of blacks in the military: let the rest of American society open its doors to African Americans and give them the opportunity they now enjoy in the armed forces."

Unlike the Vietnam War, blacks in the Gulf War did not suffer casualties at a rate greater than that for their white comrades. After less than a week of ground fighting, Iraqis agreed to a cease-fire, ending the "One Hundred–Hour War" of February 24–28. American losses were 182 dead, compared with thousands of Iraqi casualties, and only 15 percent of American fatalities in the Gulf were black. Soldiers, black and white, men and women, received a hero's welcome upon their return, as America lauded its victorious and fully integrated armed forces.

BLACK SOLDIERS' SACRIFICES and courage over the centuries have yielded significant results. Today the armed services offer African Americans greater opportunities for advancement and recognition than ever before, in addition to a commitment to reducing racism within their ranks. An Assistant Secretary of Defense reported in 1991, "The military was the first major American institution to adopt and implement equal opportunity. . . .

A black soldier poses in Kuwait next to the slogan "Honor and Courage."

U.S. MILITARY HISTORY INSTITUTE

It was not surprising that the Joint Chiefs of Staff had a black chairman before any Fortune 500 company had a black chief executive."

But remnants of racism persist. Former airborne ranger Fred Black, who in 1969 was in combat in Vietnam before going on to serve as an instructor at West Point, reminds his comrades and fellow citizens to remain steadfast in their opposition to racial discrimination: "The supreme danger is that we become complacent and believe the war is won. Battles have been won but the war continues." In this fight for racial justice, as in battles to protect and serve the nation, the black soldier continues to remain on the front lines.

Black Soldiers Past and Future

✯ ✯ ✯ ✯ ✯ ✯ ✯ ✯ ✯ ✯ ✯ ✯

IT WAS A WARM SPRING DAY in 1994 when the former general began his commencement speech to the graduating class at Howard University, one of the oldest and most prestigious black colleges. (It was named after white commander General O. O. Howard, who headed the Freedmen's Bureau, a branch of the military established to help ex-slaves and refugees during the American Civil War.) The students sat spellbound, listening to this formidable patriot, who was voted one of the most admired Americans in national polls—General Colin Powell. The Gulf War veteran proudly told his audience: "I stand here today as a direct descendant of those Buffalo Soldiers and of the Tuskegee Airmen and all the black men and women who have served the nation in uniform. I will never forget my debt to them."

Powell was acknowledging his role in a tradition of black military pioneers. These heroes range from the unheralded and often unnamed Africans who ventured to the Americas before the United States was founded to black patriots whose courage and service advanced America's cause in wars at home and abroad. Like Charles Young and Benjamin O. Davis (Sr. and Jr.), they were path breakers who earned promotion and

Colin Powell delivering a commencement address at Howard University.

MARVIN T. JONES, COURTESY OF HOWARD UNIVERSITY

advancement, overcoming great obstacles in their struggle for success. They were soldiers who fought for their country in wartime, and for dignity and justice during peacetime.

Powell clearly recognized that without the groundbreaking careers of forerunners like Young and the Davises, his climb up the ladder would have been much harder. It took generations of courageous black soldiers to force America to fulfill its promise of greatness. Consequently, the United States military became the first major American institution to promise equal opportunities and to establish and enforce policies against racial discrimination.

The progress of the black soldier remains full of twists and turns along the road to full and equal opportunity. Similarly, the path toward the just and fair recognition of achievements has also been hazardous. But the black soldier has served with pride under the stars and stripes, in peace and in war. Whatever may come, history shows us that the black soldier valiantly marches on.

U.S. MILITARY HISTORY INSTITUTE

Selected Sources

Astor, Gerald. *The Right to Fight: A History of African Americans in the Military*. Novato, Calif.: Presidio Press, 1988.

Donaldson, Gary. *The History of African Americans in the Military*. Malabar, Fla.: Krieger Publishing Co., 1991.

Foner, Jack D. *Blacks and the Military in American History*. New York: Praeger, 1974.

Glatthaar, Joseph T. *Forged in Battle: The Civil War Alliance of Black Soldiers and White Officers*. New York: Free Press, 1990.

Lanning, Michael Lee, ed. *The African-American Soldier: From Crispus Attucks to Colin Powell*. New York: Birch Lane Press, 1997.

Lindenmeyer, Otto J. *Black and Brave: The Black Soldier in America*. New York: McGraw-Hill, 1970.

McPherson, James. *The Negro's Civil War: How American Blacks Felt and Acted During the War for the Union.* 1965. Reprint ed., New York: Ballantine Books, 1991.

Nalty, Bernard C. *Strength for the Fight: A History of Black Americans in the Military.* New York: Free Press, 1986.

Quarles, Benjamin. *The Negro in the American Revolution.* 1940. Reprint ed., Chapel Hill: University of North Carolina, 1996.

————. *The Negro in the Civil War.* 1953. Reprint ed., New York: Da Capo Press, 1989.

Schubert, Frank N. *Black Valor: Buffalo Soldiers and the Medal of Honor, 1870–1898.* Wilmington, Del.: Scholarly Resources, 1997.

Index

★ ★ ★ ★ ★ ★ ★ ★ ★ ★ ★ ★ ★

FAIRBURN-HOBGOOD PALMER

J
355
CLINTON

Clinton, Catherine, 1952-

The Black soldier

Atlanta-Fulton Public Library